The Art of Letting Go: A Guide to Finding Freedom

Barbara Smith

Published by RWG Publishing, 2023.

THE ART OF LETTING GO: A GUIDE TO FINDING FREEDOM

First edition. February 21, 2023.

Copyright © 2023 Barbara Smith.

ISBN: 979-8215827635

Written by Barbara Smith.

Also by Barbara Smith

Table of Contents

The Power of Letting Go: Why It Matters

The power of letting go is one of the most transformative forces in our lives. It is a force that can free us from the shackles of our past, help us overcome our fears, and lead us towards a brighter future. Whether it is letting go of a past relationship, a long-held grudge, or simply a negative thought, the ability to release our attachments and embrace change is a crucial component of our well-being.

At its core, the power of letting go is about surrendering control. It is about relinquishing the need to hold onto things that are no longer serving us and allowing ourselves to be present in the moment. For many of us, this can be a difficult concept to grasp. We live in a society that values the accumulation of wealth, possessions, and status, and we are constantly bombarded with messages that reinforce the idea that we need more to be happy. We are told that if we can just achieve that promotion, buy that house, or find that perfect partner, we will finally be fulfilled.

However, the truth is that these things, while they may bring us temporary happiness, do not provide the lasting sense of contentment and peace that we are all searching for. In fact, the opposite is often true. When we hold onto our attachments too tightly, we can become trapped in a cycle of stress, anxiety, and dissatisfaction. We may feel a sense of emptiness or longing, as if something is missing from our lives. We may even become fearful of change, clinging to our past experiences as a means of avoiding the unknown.

The power of letting go is about breaking free from this cycle. It is about recognizing that true happiness and contentment come from within, rather than from external sources. When we let go of our attachments and surrender our need for control, we open ourselves up to new experiences, new perspectives, and new opportunities. We become more flexible, more adaptable, and more resilient, able to weather life's ups and downs with greater ease.

One of the most powerful benefits of letting go is the sense of freedom it brings. When we release our attachments, we are no longer bound by the past or beholden to the future. We can simply be present in the moment, experiencing life as it unfolds. This sense of freedom can be incredibly liberating, allowing us to live our lives on our own terms and find a sense of inner peace that transcends our external circumstances.

The power of letting go can also have a profound impact on our relationships. When we hold onto our attachments too tightly, we can become possessive, jealous, and controlling. We may struggle to communicate our needs and desires, or become defensive and argumentative when our expectations are not met. However, when we learn to let go of our attachments, we become more open and compassionate towards others. We are better able to listen, empathize, and connect with those around us, fostering deeper and more meaningful relationships.

Of course, letting go is not always easy. It can be a painful and challenging process, requiring us to confront our deepest fears and vulnerabilities. It may require us to forgive those who have hurt us, to release our regrets and resentments, or to simply accept that some things are beyond our control. However, the rewards of letting go are immeasurable. By embracing the power of letting go, we can free ourselves from the limitations of our past and create a brighter future for ourselves and those around us.

In conclusion, the power of letting go is an essential component of our well-being. It is a force that can help us break free from our attachments, surrender our need for control, and find a sense of freedom and peace that transcends our external circumstances. While it may be challenging at times, the rewards of letting go are immeasurable. By embracing the power of letting go, we can create space for new experiences, new perspectives, and new opportunities in our lives. We can cultivate deeper and more meaningful relationships with those around us, and live our lives with greater purpose and fulfillment. Whether it is letting go of a past relationship, a long-held grudge, or simply a negative thought, the power of letting go can transform our lives in ways we never thought possible.

So, if you find yourself struggling to let go of something, remember that it is a process. It may not happen overnight, and it may not be easy. But with time, patience, and perseverance, you can learn to release your attachments and embrace change. You can find a sense of inner peace and freedom that transcends your external circumstances, and live your life with greater joy and purpose.

In the next chapter, we will explore some practical strategies for letting go, including forgiveness, acceptance, and mindfulness. We will also discuss some common obstacles to letting go, such as fear, attachment, and resistance, and explore ways to overcome them. By the end of this book, you will have a comprehensive guide to the art of letting go, and the tools you need to find freedom, fulfillment, and happiness in your life.

Why We Hold On: The Psychology of Attachment

Why is it so hard to let go? What makes us cling to our past experiences, our possessions, and our relationships, even when they no longer serve us? The answer lies in the psychology of attachment, a complex web of emotions, thoughts, and behaviors that influence our relationships with ourselves and others.

At its core, attachment is a fundamental human need. From the moment we are born, we seek out connection and interaction with others, forming bonds that shape our development and well-being. These bonds can take many forms, from the nurturing relationship between a mother and child to the deep connections we form with our friends, partners, and family members. They provide us with a sense of safety, security, and comfort, and allow us to navigate the complex social world around us.

However, attachment can also be a source of pain and suffering. When we form attachments to people, things, or experiences, we become invested in them emotionally, mentally, and sometimes even physically. We become attached to the idea of what they represent to us, and may struggle to let go when they no longer serve us. This attachment can take many forms, from the sentimental attachment we have to our childhood toys, to the deep emotional attachment we have to a past relationship.

The psychology of attachment can help us understand why we hold on to things, even when they no longer serve us. According to attachment theory, our attachments are shaped by a complex interplay of emotions, experiences, and beliefs that begin in childhood and continue throughout our lives. These attachments can be healthy or unhealthy, depending on how they are formed and maintained.

One of the primary drivers of attachment is our need for safety and security. When we form attachments to people or things, we create a sense of predictability and stability in our lives. We know that we can count on these things to be there for us, and this creates a sense of comfort and security that can be difficult to let go of. This is especially true for people who have experienced trauma or loss, as attachment can become a way of coping with the uncertainty and unpredictability of the world around them.

Another factor that drives attachment is our need for self-esteem and validation. When we form attachments to people, things, or experiences that we associate with positive qualities, we enhance our own sense of self-worth. For example, we may feel more confident and capable when we are attached to a successful partner or job, or we may feel more secure when we are attached to a certain set of possessions or experiences. These attachments can become a source of validation and self-esteem, making it difficult to let go even when they no longer serve us.

Finally, attachment can be driven by our beliefs and values. We form attachments to things that we believe are important, whether it is a sentimental object from our past or a deeply held belief about the world around us. These attachments can be deeply ingrained, and may be difficult to let go of because they are so closely tied to our sense of identity and purpose.

In conclusion, the psychology of attachment plays a powerful role in shaping our relationships with ourselves and others. It influences our need for safety, security, validation, and meaning, and can create deep emotional ties that are difficult to break. However, by understanding the nature of attachment and the factors that drive it, we can begin to let go of attachments that no longer serve us, and cultivate healthier, more fulfilling relationships with ourselves and those around us. In the next chapter, we will explore some practical strategies for letting go of attachments, including mindfulness, self-compassion, and cognitive restructuring. By developing a deeper understanding of attachment and learning to let go of unhealthy attachments, we can create space for new experiences, new relationships, and a greater sense of fulfillment and purpose in our lives.

The Freedom in Forgiveness

Forgiveness is one of the most powerful tools we have for finding freedom in our lives. It allows us to release the negative emotions and thoughts that are holding us back, and to move forward with a greater sense of peace, compassion, and understanding. However, forgiveness is not always easy. It requires us to confront our own pain and anger, and to find a way to let go of our attachment to the past. In this chapter, we will explore the freedom that comes with forgiveness, and some of the strategies we can use to cultivate forgiveness in our lives.

At its core, forgiveness is about releasing ourselves from the pain and suffering caused by the actions of others. It is about finding a way to move past the hurt and anger that we may feel towards someone who has wronged us, and to find a place of compassion and understanding. Forgiveness does not mean forgetting or condoning the actions of others, but rather, it is a way of finding peace within ourselves and freeing ourselves from the negative emotions that are holding us back.

One of the key benefits of forgiveness is the sense of freedom that it brings. When we hold on to anger, resentment, and bitterness towards someone else, we are essentially giving them power over our lives. We are allowing their actions to control our emotions and thoughts, and to shape our experiences of the world around us. By forgiving, we take back that power, and we free ourselves from the negative emotions that are holding us back.

Forgiveness also allows us to see the world with greater clarity and compassion. When we are trapped in feelings of anger and resentment, we may see the world through a lens of negativity and bitterness. This can create a self-fulfilling cycle of negativity, where we continue to attract negative experiences into our lives. By forgiving, we release ourselves from this cycle, and we open ourselves up to new experiences and opportunities for growth and healing.

So, how can we cultivate forgiveness in our lives? One approach is to begin with self-forgiveness. Often, our inability to forgive others is rooted in our own self-judgment and self-criticism. By learning to forgive ourselves for our own mistakes and shortcomings, we can develop greater compassion and understanding for others.

Another approach is to focus on empathy and understanding. When we can see the world through the eyes of another person, we are better able to understand their actions and motivations. This can help us to release our own feelings of anger and resentment, and to find a place of compassion and understanding.

It is also important to practice self-care and self-compassion as we work towards forgiveness. Forgiveness can be a difficult and emotional process, and it is important to be kind to ourselves as we navigate this journey. This may involve seeking support from friends, family members, or a therapist, or engaging in activities that bring us joy and relaxation.

In conclusion, forgiveness is a powerful tool for finding freedom in our lives. It allows us to release ourselves from the negative emotions and thoughts that are holding us back, and to find a place of peace, compassion, and understanding. By cultivating forgiveness in our lives, we can free ourselves from the past, and create space for new experiences, new relationships, and a greater sense of fulfillment and purpose. In the next chapter, we will explore some practical strategies for forgiveness, including meditation, journaling, and cognitive restructuring. By learning to forgive, we can find a greater sense of freedom, happiness, and fulfillment in our lives.

Navigating Grief and Loss with Grace

Grief and loss are a natural part of the human experience, and they can be some of the most difficult challenges we face in life. Whether we are dealing with the loss of a loved one, the end of a relationship, or a major life change, the emotions that come with grief can be overwhelming and intense. In this chapter, we will explore some of the strategies for navigating grief and loss with grace, and finding a sense of peace and acceptance in the midst of difficult times.

One of the first steps in navigating grief and loss is to allow ourselves to feel the emotions that come with it. This may include feelings of sadness, anger, guilt, and even relief. It is important to acknowledge these emotions and to give ourselves permission to experience them, rather than trying to suppress them or push them away. This can be a challenging process, but it is an important step in the journey towards healing.

Another key strategy for navigating grief and loss is to practice self-compassion. This involves being kind and gentle with ourselves as we go through the grieving process, and giving ourselves the space and time we need to heal. This may involve taking time off work or other responsibilities, engaging in self-care activities like exercise or meditation, or seeking support from friends, family, or a therapist.

It is also important to find ways to honor the memory of the person or thing we have lost. This may involve creating a memorial or tribute, engaging in rituals or traditions that have personal significance, or finding ways to continue to connect with the person or thing in a meaningful way. By finding ways to honor the memory of what we have lost, we can create a sense of continuity and connection, even in the midst of change and loss.

Another important strategy for navigating grief and loss is to seek out support from others. This may involve reaching out to friends or family members, or joining a support group for people who are going through similar experiences. It can also be helpful to work with a therapist or counselor, who can provide a safe and supportive space for processing emotions and working through the grieving process.

Finally, it is important to remember that the process of grieving is not linear or predictable. It can involve a range of emotions, including setbacks and relapses, and it may take longer than we expect. It is important to give ourselves the space and time we need to heal, and to be patient and kind with ourselves as we navigate the ups and downs of the grieving process.

In conclusion, navigating grief and loss with grace requires a combination of self-compassion, support from others, and strategies for honoring the memory of what we have lost. By allowing ourselves to feel the emotions that come with grief, practicing self-care and self-compassion, seeking out support from others, and finding ways to honor the memory of what we have lost, we can find a sense of peace and acceptance in the midst of difficult times. While the journey towards healing may be challenging, it is possible to find a way through the grief and come out on the other side with a greater sense of resilience, strength, and compassion.

Embracing Change: A Guide to Letting Go of the Familiar

C hange is a constant in life, and yet it is often met with resistance and fear. Whether it's a change in our personal lives or a change in the world around us, we often cling to the familiar and resist the unknown. In this chapter, we will explore the importance of embracing change and letting go of the familiar, and provide a guide for navigating the challenges that come with it.

The first step in embracing change is to acknowledge and accept that it is a natural and necessary part of life. Change can bring new opportunities for growth and learning, and it can help us to develop resilience and adaptability. When we resist change, we close ourselves off from these opportunities and limit our potential for growth.

One of the main reasons we resist change is that it can be uncomfortable and uncertain. It can challenge our sense of control and stability, and it can bring up feelings of anxiety and fear. However, it is important to recognize that these feelings are a natural part of the process, and that they can be managed with the right mindset and tools.

One key strategy for embracing change is to focus on the positive aspects of the change. This may involve identifying the opportunities and potential benefits that the change could bring, or finding ways to reframe our perspective to see the change as a positive step forward. By focusing on the positive, we can begin to shift our mindset from one of fear and resistance to one of openness and possibility.

Another important strategy for embracing change is to practice self-care and self-compassion. Change can be a stressful and emotionally challenging time, and it is important to take care of ourselves during the process. This may involve engaging in activities that help to reduce stress and promote relaxation, such as exercise, meditation, or spending time in nature. It can also involve seeking out support from friends, family, or a therapist, who can provide a safe and supportive space for processing emotions and working through the challenges that come with change.

It is also important to be patient and flexible during the process of change. Change is not always predictable or linear, and it may involve setbacks and challenges along the way. By staying patient and flexible, we can remain open to new possibilities and opportunities, and find creative solutions to the challenges that arise.

Finally, it is important to celebrate our successes and accomplishments along the way. Embracing change is not always easy, and it can involve a lot of hard work and effort. By taking the time to acknowledge and celebrate the progress we have made, we can build confidence and resilience, and stay motivated to continue moving forward.

In conclusion, embracing change is an important part of life, and it can bring new opportunities for growth and learning. By focusing on the positive aspects of the change, practicing self-care and self-compassion, staying patient and flexible, and celebrating our successes along the way, we can navigate the challenges that come with change and emerge stronger and more resilient on the other side. While change may be uncomfortable and uncertain, it is important to remember that it is also a natural and necessary part of life, and that it can bring new opportunities and possibilities that we may never have imagined otherwise.

Learning to Release Control: How to Find Trust in the Unknown

A s human beings, we crave control. We want to know what is going to happen, when it is going to happen, and how it is going to happen. This need for control can bring a sense of security and stability, but it can also create stress and anxiety, especially when we are faced with situations that are beyond our control. In this chapter, we will explore the importance of releasing control and finding trust in the unknown, and provide a guide for navigating the challenges that come with it.

The first step in learning to release control is to acknowledge and accept that there are many things in life that are beyond our control. While we may be able to influence certain outcomes through our thoughts and actions, there are many factors that are outside of our sphere of influence. It is important to recognize that this lack of control is a natural and inevitable part of life, and that it can bring new opportunities for growth and learning.

One of the main reasons we cling to control is that it can create a sense of security and predictability. When we feel in control, we feel like we can predict what is going to happen and prepare accordingly. However, it is important to recognize that this sense of security is often illusory, and that it can create more stress and anxiety in the long run. By learning to release control and find trust in the unknown, we can cultivate a sense of peace and equanimity, even in the face of uncertainty.

One key strategy for releasing control is to practice mindfulness and presence. By staying present in the moment and focusing on what is happening right now, we can reduce our tendency to worry about the future or dwell on the past. This can help us to stay calm and centered, even in the midst of uncertainty.

Another important strategy for releasing control is to cultivate a sense of trust and faith in the unknown. This may involve developing a spiritual practice, or simply cultivating a sense of trust in the universe or a higher power. By trusting in something greater than ourselves, we can find a sense of peace and equanimity, even in the face of uncertainty.

It is also important to practice self-compassion and self-care during the process of releasing control. This may involve engaging in activities that help to reduce stress and promote relaxation, such as exercise, meditation, or spending time in nature. It can also involve seeking out support from friends, family, or a therapist, who can provide a safe and supportive space for processing emotions and working through the challenges that come with releasing control.

Finally, it is important to approach the process of releasing control with a sense of curiosity and openness. Instead of viewing uncertainty as a threat, we can view it as an opportunity for growth and learning. By staying curious and open to new possibilities, we can cultivate a sense of excitement and wonder about what the future may hold.

In conclusion, releasing control is an important part of finding trust in the unknown, and it can bring a sense of peace and equanimity, even in the face of uncertainty. By practicing mindfulness and presence, cultivating a sense of trust and faith, practicing self-compassion and self-care, and approaching the process with a sense of curiosity and openness, we can learn to release control and find trust in the unknown. While it may be challenging to let go of our need for control, it is important to remember that this is a natural and inevitable part of life, and that it can bring new opportunities and possibilities that we may never have imagined otherwise. By embracing the unknown and finding trust in the process, we can cultivate a sense of peace and equanimity that will serve us well throughout our lives.

Letting Go of Resentment: Finding Peace in Conflict

Resentment is a common emotion that arises in many conflicts, and it can be a significant obstacle to finding resolution and peace. When we hold onto feelings of anger and bitterness, it can cloud our judgment and prevent us from seeing the situation clearly. In this chapter, we will explore the importance of letting go of resentment in conflict, and provide a guide for finding peace and resolution.

The first step in letting go of resentment is to acknowledge and accept our feelings. It is natural to feel angry or hurt when we have been wronged, and it is important to allow ourselves to feel these emotions without judgment. However, it is also important to recognize that holding onto these emotions can create more suffering in the long run, and prevent us from finding resolution and peace.

One key strategy for letting go of resentment is to practice forgiveness. Forgiveness does not mean condoning the actions of the other person, or forgetting what happened. Rather, it is a process of releasing our own negative emotions and choosing to let go of the past. Forgiveness can be a powerful tool for finding peace and resolution in conflict, and it can help to restore trust and connection in relationships.

Another important strategy for letting go of resentment is to focus on our own needs and values. When we are in conflict, it can be easy to get caught up in the other person's perspective and lose sight of our own needs and values. By focusing on our own needs and values, we can create a sense of clarity and purpose, and find new opportunities for growth and learning.

It is also important to communicate clearly and respectfully during the process of letting go of resentment. When we are in conflict, it can be easy to become defensive or aggressive, which can escalate the situation and create more tension. By communicating in a clear and respectful way, we can create a safe and supportive space for dialogue and understanding.

Finally, it is important to practice self-compassion and self-care during the process of letting go of resentment. Conflict can be stressful and emotionally taxing, and it is important to take care of ourselves during this time. This may involve engaging in activities that promote relaxation and reduce stress, such as exercise, meditation, or spending time in nature. It can also involve seeking out support from friends, family, or a therapist, who can provide a safe and supportive space for processing emotions and working through the challenges that come with letting go of resentment.

In conclusion, letting go of resentment is an important part of finding peace and resolution in conflict, and it can help to restore trust and connection in relationships. By acknowledging and accepting our emotions, practicing forgiveness, focusing on our own needs and values, communicating clearly and respectfully, and practicing self-compassion and self-care, we can learn to let go of resentment and find new opportunities for growth and learning. While it may be challenging to release our negative emotions and find peace in conflict, it is important to remember that this process can bring a sense of peace and healing that will serve us well throughout our lives. By embracing the process of letting go and finding new opportunities for growth and learning, we can cultivate a sense of resilience and empowerment that will serve us well in all areas of our lives.

The Art of Saying Goodbye: How to End Relationships Gracefully

Saying goodbye is an inevitable part of life, and it can be a challenging and emotional process, particularly when it comes to ending relationships. Whether we are ending a romantic relationship, a friendship, or a professional partnership, it is important to do so in a way that is respectful, compassionate, and graceful. In this chapter, we will explore the art of saying goodbye, and provide a guide for ending relationships with grace.

The first step in ending a relationship gracefully is to reflect on our reasons for doing so. It is important to be clear and honest with ourselves about why we feel it is time to move on, and to communicate this in a respectful and compassionate way. This may involve acknowledging our own role in the relationship and taking responsibility for any mistakes or shortcomings, as well as recognizing the other person's perspective and feelings.

Once we have reflected on our reasons for ending the relationship, the next step is to communicate this to the other person in a clear and respectful way. This may involve having a conversation in person or over the phone, or sending a message or email if it is not possible to meet in person. It is important to be direct and honest, while also being compassionate and considerate of the other person's feelings.

During the process of ending a relationship, it is also important to listen to the other person's perspective and feelings. This may involve allowing them to express their own thoughts and emotions, without judgment or defensiveness. It may also involve acknowledging their own role in the relationship, and expressing gratitude for the positive aspects of the relationship.

Another key strategy for ending a relationship gracefully is to create closure and a sense of completion. This may involve expressing appreciation for the time spent together, and acknowledging the positive aspects of the relationship. It may also involve finding ways to create a sense of closure, such as exchanging a final goodbye or symbolic gesture, or engaging in a ritual or ceremony to mark the end of the relationship.

Finally, it is important to take care of ourselves during the process of ending a relationship. This may involve seeking support from friends, family, or a therapist, who can provide a safe and supportive space for processing emotions and working through the challenges that come with saying goodbye. It may also involve engaging in activities that promote self-care and self-compassion, such as exercise, meditation, or spending time in nature.

In conclusion, the art of saying goodbye is an important skill for ending relationships gracefully and with compassion. By reflecting on our reasons for ending the relationship, communicating clearly and respectfully, listening to the other person's perspective and feelings, creating closure, and taking care of ourselves, we can find a way to say goodbye that is respectful and compassionate, while also allowing us to move forward with grace and dignity. While saying goodbye may be a challenging and emotional process, it is important to remember that it can also be a powerful opportunity for growth and learning, and for creating new opportunities for connection and healing in the future. By embracing the process of saying goodbye and finding new opportunities for growth and learning, we can cultivate a sense of resilience and empowerment that will serve us well in all areas of our lives.

The Courage to Let Go: Overcoming Fear and Doubt

L etting go of something that has been a significant part of our lives, whether it be a person, a job, or a belief, can be a difficult and challenging experience. It can require us to step outside of our comfort zones and face our fears and doubts. In this chapter, we will explore the courage to let go and provide strategies for overcoming fear and doubt.

One of the first steps in letting go is acknowledging and accepting the emotions that arise when we consider releasing something that has been a significant part of our lives. Fear, doubt, and uncertainty are common emotions that arise when we contemplate letting go of something familiar. It's important to recognize that these emotions are natural and that we don't need to feel ashamed of them. Instead, we can acknowledge them and use them as a source of motivation to take action.

The second step is to assess the situation and determine what we stand to gain by letting go. It can be helpful to focus on the positive outcomes of releasing what we are holding onto. This can include gaining new opportunities, personal growth, and increased freedom. Focusing on the benefits of letting go can help us shift our mindset from one of fear and doubt to one of possibility and hope.

The third step is to create a plan of action. This can include setting goals and taking small steps towards releasing what we are holding onto. Breaking down the process into manageable tasks can help us to overcome feelings of overwhelm and uncertainty. By taking action, we can build momentum and increase our confidence in our ability to let go.

The fourth step is to seek support. It can be helpful to surround ourselves with people who are supportive and understanding of our decision to let go. Friends, family members, or a therapist can provide a safe and non-judgmental space to process emotions and receive guidance and support.

The fifth step is to practice self-compassion. Letting go of something that has been a significant part of our lives can be an emotional and challenging process. It's important to be kind and gentle with ourselves and acknowledge that we are doing the best we can. It's also important to recognize that we may experience setbacks and to be patient with ourselves as we work through the process of letting go.

Finally, it's important to recognize that letting go is not a one-time event, but rather a process that requires ongoing effort and commitment. We may need to revisit our decision to let go and remind ourselves of the reasons why we made the decision in the first place. We may also need to continue to work through our emotions and seek support as we navigate the challenges of letting go.

In conclusion, the courage to let go requires us to face our fears and doubts and to take action towards releasing what we are holding onto. By acknowledging and accepting our emotions, focusing on the positive outcomes of letting go, creating a plan of action, seeking support, practicing self-compassion, and recognizing that letting go is an ongoing process, we can cultivate the courage and resilience needed to move forward with grace and confidence. While letting go may be a challenging and emotional process, it is also an opportunity for growth and transformation, and for creating new opportunities for connection and healing in the future. By embracing the process of letting go and finding the courage to release what no longer serves us, we can create a life that is rich with possibility, growth, and meaning.

Letting Go of Perfection: The Joy of Embracing Imperfection

Perfectionism is a trait that is often associated with high achievement and success. However, the pursuit of perfection can also lead to stress, anxiety, and a sense of never feeling good enough. In this chapter, we will explore the concept of letting go of perfection and the joy that can be found in embracing imperfection.

Perfectionism is the belief that one must be flawless and perfect in order to be valued and accepted. This belief can be a double-edged sword, as it can motivate us to strive for excellence, but it can also lead to self-criticism, self-doubt, and a sense of never measuring up. The pursuit of perfection can also lead to a rigid mindset, where mistakes are seen as failures rather than opportunities for learning and growth.

The first step in letting go of perfection is to recognize the negative impact that it has on our lives. This can include increased stress and anxiety, decreased productivity, and a sense of feeling overwhelmed and burned out. Once we acknowledge the negative impact of perfectionism, we can start to explore the benefits of embracing imperfection.

Embracing imperfection means accepting ourselves and others as we are, flaws and all. It means recognizing that mistakes and failures are a natural part of the learning process and that they can be valuable opportunities for growth and development. Embracing imperfection can also lead to increased creativity, spontaneity, and a sense of playfulness and joy.

The second step in letting go of perfection is to cultivate self-compassion. Self-compassion means treating ourselves with kindness and understanding, rather than self-criticism and self-blame. It means recognizing that we are human and that we are not perfect. Practicing self-compassion can help us to let go of the unrealistic expectations that we place on ourselves and to embrace imperfection with an open heart and mind.

The third step is to shift our mindset from one of all-or-nothing thinking to one of progress, not perfection. This means focusing on the process of growth and development, rather than the end result. It means recognizing that progress is not always linear and that setbacks and failures are a natural part of the journey. By embracing progress, not perfection, we can let go of the pressure to be flawless and instead focus on the joy of learning and growing.

The fourth step is to surround ourselves with supportive and understanding people. It can be helpful to connect with others who have also struggled with perfectionism and who can provide a safe and non-judgmental space to share our experiences and receive guidance and support.

The fifth step is to practice self-care and self-acceptance. This can include engaging in activities that bring us joy and fulfillment, such as hobbies, exercise, or spending time with loved ones. It can also include practicing mindfulness and self-reflection, and recognizing our strengths and talents, as well as our limitations and areas for growth.

In conclusion, letting go of perfection requires us to embrace imperfection and to cultivate self-compassion, progress, and self-acceptance. By recognizing the negative impact of perfectionism and the benefits of embracing imperfection, we can shift our mindset and find joy in the journey of growth and development. By surrounding ourselves with supportive and understanding people and engaging in self-care and self-reflection, we can create a life that is rich with meaning, joy, and fulfillment. While letting go of perfection may be a challenging process, it is also an opportunity for growth, creativity, and self-discovery. By letting go of the need to be flawless and embracing imperfection with an open heart and mind, we can create a life that is rich with joy, connection, and meaning.

Healing Through Letting Go: How to Find Closure and Move On

Letting go can be a difficult process, especially when it comes to emotional pain and past traumas. However, the process of healing often requires us to let go of the past in order to move forward and find closure. In this chapter, we will explore the concept of healing through letting go, and provide practical tips and strategies for finding closure and moving on.

The first step in healing through letting go is to acknowledge the pain and emotions associated with the past. It is important to allow ourselves to feel the emotions associated with past traumas, rather than suppressing or avoiding them. This can be a difficult process, as it often requires us to confront difficult emotions, memories, and experiences. However, by acknowledging and processing these emotions, we can begin to move towards healing and closure.

The second step is to identify what we need to let go of in order to move forward. This can include toxic relationships, unhealthy patterns of behavior, or past traumas that continue to impact our daily lives. It can be helpful to write down a list of what we need to let go of in order to move forward, and to create a plan for doing so.

The third step is to practice forgiveness. Forgiveness does not mean condoning or excusing past behavior, but rather acknowledging the harm that was done and choosing to let go of resentment and anger. This can be a difficult process, especially when it comes to past traumas or experiences that have deeply hurt us. However, practicing forgiveness can be a powerful tool in the process of healing and finding closure.

The fourth step is to practice self-care and self-compassion. This can include engaging in activities that bring us joy and fulfillment, such as hobbies, exercise, or spending time with loved ones. It can also include practicing mindfulness and self-reflection, and recognizing our strengths and talents, as well as our limitations and areas for growth. By taking care of ourselves and showing ourselves compassion, we can begin to heal and find closure.

The fifth step is to seek support and guidance from others. This can include therapy, support groups, or trusted friends and family members. It can be helpful to connect with others who have also experienced similar struggles, and who can provide a safe and non-judgmental space to share our experiences and receive guidance and support.

The sixth step is to focus on the present moment and future. Letting go of the past does not mean forgetting about it, but rather accepting it and moving forward. It is important to focus on the present moment and future, and to set goals and intentions for what we want to create in our lives. By focusing on the present moment and future, we can create a sense of purpose and direction, and move towards a life that is rich with meaning and fulfillment.

In conclusion, healing through letting go requires us to acknowledge and process our emotions, identify what we need to let go of in order to move forward, practice forgiveness and self-care, seek support and guidance from others, and focus on the present moment and future. While the process of healing through letting go can be difficult and challenging, it is also an opportunity for growth, self-discovery, and transformation. By letting go of the past and finding closure, we can create a life that is rich with meaning, joy, and fulfillment. By acknowledging our pain and emotions, practicing forgiveness and self-care, and seeking support from others, we can begin to heal and find closure. By focusing on the present moment and future, and setting goals and intentions for what we want to create in our lives, we can move towards a life that is rich with purpose and direction. Ultimately, healing through letting go is a journey that requires patience, self-compassion, and the courage to embrace change and transformation.

Finding Gratitude in Letting Go: Why We Should Celebrate Our Freedom

Letting go can be a difficult and sometimes painful process, but it can also be a powerful opportunity for growth, transformation, and freedom. By letting go of what no longer serves us, we create space for new experiences, relationships, and opportunities to enter our lives. In this chapter, we will explore the concept of finding gratitude in letting go, and why celebrating our freedom is an important part of the process.

When we let go of something or someone, we create a sense of liberation and freedom. We may feel a weight lifted off our shoulders, a sense of relief, or a renewed sense of purpose and direction. By embracing this sense of freedom, we open ourselves up to new possibilities and experiences that we may not have otherwise had. We can find gratitude in the opportunity to start fresh, to redefine ourselves, and to create a life that aligns with our values and passions.

Finding gratitude in letting go can also help us cultivate a positive and grateful mindset. Gratitude has been linked to numerous benefits, including improved mental and physical health, increased happiness and well-being, and stronger relationships. By focusing on what we are grateful for in the process of letting go, we can shift our mindset towards a more positive and optimistic outlook, which can help us navigate challenges and setbacks with greater resilience and determination.

Furthermore, celebrating our freedom can inspire and motivate us to pursue our dreams and aspirations. When we let go of what no longer serves us, we create space for new opportunities to enter our lives. This can be an exciting and invigorating time, as we explore new paths and possibilities. By celebrating our freedom, we can tap into a sense of courage, creativity, and inspiration that can help us pursue our goals and dreams with greater confidence and determination.

It is also important to recognize that finding gratitude in letting go is not about minimizing the challenges or pain associated with the process. Letting go can be a difficult and emotional process, and it is important to honor and acknowledge the full range of emotions that come with it. However, by focusing on what we are grateful for in the process, we can find meaning and purpose in the journey, and recognize the opportunities for growth and transformation that it presents.

So how can we find gratitude in letting go? Here are a few practical tips and strategies:

Reflect on what you are grateful for in the present moment. This can include relationships, experiences, opportunities, or qualities that you appreciate in yourself or others. By focusing on what you are grateful for in the present, you can cultivate a sense of abundance and positivity that can help you navigate the process of letting go with greater resilience and determination.

Keep a gratitude journal. Write down three things that you are grateful for each day, including specific moments, experiences, or people that you appreciate. By reflecting on what you are grateful for on a regular basis, you can cultivate a more positive and grateful mindset that can help you navigate challenges and setbacks with greater resilience and determination.

Practice self-compassion. Letting go can be a difficult and emotional process, and it is important to show yourself compassion and kindness throughout the journey. Be patient with yourself, acknowledge and honor the full range of emotions that come with letting go, and celebrate the progress and growth that you have made.

In conclusion, finding gratitude in letting go can be a powerful tool for growth, transformation, and freedom. By celebrating our freedom, we open ourselves up to new possibilities and experiences, cultivate a positive and grateful mindset, and tap into a sense of courage, creativity, and inspiration that can help us pursue our goals and dreams with greater confidence and determination. By reflecting on what we are grateful for in the present moment, keeping a gratitude journal, and practicing self-compassion, we can find meaning and purpose in the journey of letting go, and recognize the opportunities for growth and transformation that it presents.

As you navigate the process of letting go, it is important to remember that finding gratitude is a personal and ongoing journey. What works for one person may not work for another, and the process may ebb and flow as you move through different stages of growth and transformation. However, by remaining open and curious, and by focusing on what you are grateful for in the present moment, you can cultivate a sense of freedom, abundance, and joy that can help you navigate the challenges and opportunities of life with greater resilience and determination.

Ultimately, finding gratitude in letting go is about embracing the power of the present moment and recognizing the beauty and potential that lies within it. By celebrating your freedom, you can cultivate a sense of purpose and direction, and tap into the courage and inspiration that you need to pursue your goals and dreams with greater passion and determination. So take a moment to reflect on what you are grateful for in the process of letting go, and allow yourself to embrace the power and beauty of the present moment.

Moving Beyond Regret: How to Forgive Yourself and Others

Regret can be a heavy burden to carry, weighing down our spirits and preventing us from moving forward in life. Whether it is regret over past mistakes, missed opportunities, or hurtful actions, the pain of regret can be difficult to overcome. However, by learning to forgive yourself and others, you can move beyond regret and find peace and freedom in the present moment.

Forgiveness is a powerful tool for healing and growth, allowing us to release the past and move forward with a greater sense of purpose and direction. When we hold onto regret, we are stuck in the past, unable to fully embrace the opportunities and possibilities that exist in the present moment. By forgiving ourselves and others, we can let go of the pain and anger that we may be holding onto, and embrace a sense of compassion, empathy, and understanding that can help us find greater peace and fulfillment in life.

Forgiving yourself and others requires a willingness to let go of judgment and criticism, and to approach the situation with an open heart and mind. It is important to recognize that everyone makes mistakes, and that holding onto blame and resentment only creates more suffering for ourselves and others. By choosing to forgive, we are choosing to release ourselves from the burden of the past, and to embrace the potential for growth and transformation that lies within us.

One of the keys to forgiving yourself and others is to cultivate a sense of empathy and understanding. This means recognizing the pain and challenges that others may have faced, and choosing to respond with compassion and kindness, rather than judgment and anger. It also means acknowledging our own shortcomings and limitations, and recognizing that we are all imperfect human beings, capable of making mistakes and learning from them.

Another important aspect of forgiveness is accepting responsibility for our own actions and choices. This means acknowledging the impact that our behavior may have had on others, and choosing to take steps to make amends and repair any damage that has been done. It also means being willing to learn from our mistakes, and to make changes in our behavior and attitudes that can help us avoid making similar mistakes in the future.

Forgiving ourselves and others can be a difficult and challenging process, but it is essential for our growth and well-being. It requires a willingness to let go of the past, and to embrace the potential for growth and transformation that lies within us. By choosing to forgive, we are choosing to cultivate a sense of compassion, understanding, and empathy, and to create a brighter, more hopeful future for ourselves and others.

If you are struggling to forgive yourself or others, there are a number of strategies that can be helpful. These may include seeking the support of a trusted friend or therapist, practicing mindfulness and meditation to cultivate a greater sense of compassion and empathy, or engaging in acts of service and kindness to others as a way of cultivating a sense of gratitude and perspective.

Ultimately, the key to moving beyond regret and finding forgiveness is to approach the situation with an open heart and mind, and to recognize the potential for growth and transformation that lies within us. By choosing to forgive, we are choosing to let go of the past and embrace the beauty and potential of the present moment, and to create a brighter, more hopeful future for ourselves and others.

The Art of Detachment: Finding Balance in Relationships

One of the most challenging aspects of any relationship is finding a sense of balance and harmony. While it is natural to care deeply about those we love and to feel invested in their lives, it is also important to maintain a sense of detachment, in order to avoid becoming too enmeshed or emotionally dependent. The art of detachment is about finding a healthy balance between caring deeply and being emotionally self-sufficient, and it can be a powerful tool for building healthier, more sustainable relationships.

Detachment does not mean disengaging from our relationships, or becoming cold and distant. Rather, it means cultivating a sense of inner strength and self-awareness that allows us to engage with others from a place of groundedness and equanimity. This can help us to avoid getting too caught up in the drama or emotions of others, and to maintain a sense of perspective and objectivity that is essential for healthy relationships.

One of the key elements of detachment is setting healthy boundaries. This means being clear about our own needs and limitations, and communicating these effectively to others. It also means being willing to say no when necessary, and to prioritize our own well-being and self-care. When we set healthy boundaries, we create a sense of safety and stability that allows us to engage with others from a place of strength and confidence.

Another important aspect of detachment is cultivating a sense of self-acceptance and self-love. When we are able to love and accept ourselves, we are less likely to look to others for validation or affirmation. This can help us to avoid becoming too dependent on our relationships, and to maintain a sense of independence and self-sufficiency that is essential for healthy detachment.

Detachment also involves a willingness to let go of our attachment to specific outcomes or expectations. When we become too attached to our desires or expectations, we can become overly invested in the outcome of our relationships, and lose sight of the present moment. By letting go of our attachment to specific outcomes, we can stay present and engaged in the moment, and avoid becoming too focused on what may or may not happen in the future.

Finally, detachment involves a willingness to practice mindfulness and present moment awareness. When we are able to stay present and mindful, we are better able to observe our thoughts and emotions without becoming overwhelmed by them. This can help us to avoid becoming too attached to our own emotional responses, and to maintain a sense of equanimity and balance that is essential for healthy detachment.

In order to cultivate a sense of detachment, it is important to practice self-care and self-compassion. This may involve engaging in activities that bring us joy and fulfillment, such as hobbies, exercise, or spending time in nature. It may also involve practicing meditation or mindfulness, or seeking the support of a trusted therapist or friend.

Ultimately, the art of detachment is about finding a sense of balance and harmony in our relationships, and cultivating a sense of inner strength and self-awareness that allows us to engage with others from a place of groundedness and equanimity. By setting healthy boundaries, cultivating self-acceptance and self-love, letting go of attachment to specific outcomes, and practicing mindfulness and present moment awareness, we can build healthier, more sustainable relationships that bring us joy, fulfillment, and a sense of inner peace.

Letting Go of Judgment: How to Find Compassion and Understanding

We all have a tendency to judge others based on our own perceptions, experiences, and beliefs. Whether it's judging someone for their lifestyle choices, their appearance, or their beliefs, we often make assumptions and form opinions about others without really knowing them. However, this tendency to judge others can be detrimental to our own well-being, as well as to the quality of our relationships. Letting go of judgment and cultivating compassion and understanding can be a powerful way to enhance our relationships and promote greater happiness and fulfillment in our lives.

One of the first steps in letting go of judgment is to become aware of our own biases and assumptions. This means examining our own beliefs and values, and recognizing that they are not necessarily universal or applicable to others. It also means acknowledging the impact of our own experiences and upbringing on our perceptions of others. By becoming more aware of our own biases and assumptions, we can start to question them and develop a more open-minded and compassionate approach to others.

Another key step in letting go of judgment is to practice empathy and compassion. This means putting ourselves in the shoes of others and trying to see things from their perspective. It means acknowledging the struggles, challenges, and complexities of others' lives, and recognizing that we may not have all the information or understanding necessary to fully appreciate their experiences. When we practice empathy and compassion, we create a sense of connection and understanding that can help to bridge differences and promote greater understanding and acceptance.

Letting go of judgment also involves developing greater self-awareness and self-acceptance. When we are more accepting of ourselves and our own imperfections, we are less likely to judge others for theirs. This can help us to cultivate a more forgiving and understanding approach to others, and to develop greater empathy and compassion.

Another important step in letting go of judgment is to practice active listening. This means really listening to others and trying to understand their perspective, without interrupting, judging, or trying to impose our own views. When we practice active listening, we create a sense of safety and respect that can help to foster greater trust and understanding in our relationships.

Finally, letting go of judgment involves a willingness to challenge our own assumptions and beliefs. This means being open to new ideas and perspectives, and being willing to learn from others. It also means recognizing that our own beliefs and values are not fixed or immutable, but are constantly evolving and changing. When we are open to new ideas and perspectives, we create a sense of curiosity and humility that can help us to overcome our own biases and judgments.

In order to cultivate greater compassion and understanding, it is important to practice self-care and self-compassion. This may involve engaging in activities that bring us joy and fulfillment, such as hobbies, exercise, or spending time in nature. It may also involve practicing meditation or mindfulness, or seeking the support of a trusted therapist or friend.

Ultimately, the key to letting go of judgment is to cultivate a sense of openness and curiosity towards others. By becoming more aware of our own biases and assumptions, practicing empathy and compassion, developing self-awareness and self-acceptance, practicing active listening, and challenging our own assumptions and beliefs, we can create a more accepting and compassionate approach to others. This can help us to build deeper, more fulfilling relationships, and to experience greater happiness and well-being in our lives.

Finding Clarity in Chaos: How to Let Go of Overthinking

In today's world, it's all too easy to get caught up in the chaos of life. With constant stimulation from social media, news updates, and work deadlines, it's easy to feel overwhelmed and anxious. When we become consumed with our thoughts and worries, it can be difficult to make clear decisions and move forward in a positive way. This is where the art of letting go comes in, especially when it comes to letting go of overthinking.

Overthinking is a common issue that many people face. We may find ourselves dwelling on past mistakes, worrying about the future, or obsessing over details that we can't control. This can lead to anxiety, stress, and even depression. However, by learning to let go of overthinking, we can find clarity and peace in the midst of chaos.

The first step in letting go of overthinking is to become aware of when we're doing it. We need to recognize the patterns in our thoughts and acknowledge when we're getting caught up in a cycle of worry or anxiety. Once we're aware of the issue, we can take steps to change our thought patterns and move towards a more positive mindset.

One way to let go of overthinking is to practice mindfulness. This involves paying attention to the present moment, without judgment or distraction. By focusing on our breath, our surroundings, and our sensations, we can bring our minds back to the present and away from obsessive thoughts. Mindfulness can be practiced through meditation, yoga, or simply taking a few deep breaths when we feel our minds start to race.

Another effective way to let go of overthinking is to journal. By writing down our thoughts and feelings, we can release them from our minds and gain perspective on our worries. We can also use journaling to set intentions, reflect on our goals, and express gratitude for the things we have in our lives. Writing can be a powerful tool in finding clarity and moving forward with purpose.

In addition to mindfulness and journaling, it's important to take care of ourselves physically. Exercise, healthy eating, and getting enough sleep can all contribute to a clearer mind and a more positive outlook. By taking care of our bodies, we can give ourselves the energy and resilience we need to let go of overthinking and move forward in a positive direction.

Finally, it's important to remember that letting go of overthinking is a process. We may have days where our minds race and our worries seem overwhelming. But by practicing mindfulness, journaling, and self-care, we can gradually learn to let go of our obsessive thoughts and find clarity in the chaos. It's a journey, and it's one that requires patience and self-compassion.

In conclusion, letting go of overthinking is an essential part of the art of letting go. By becoming aware of our thoughts and practicing mindfulness, journaling, and self-care, we can release ourselves from the cycle of worry and anxiety. We can find clarity in the chaos and move forward with purpose and positivity. It's not always easy, but with practice and dedication, it's possible to let go of overthinking and find peace in our minds and hearts.

Letting Go of the Past: Why It's Important to Live in the Present

L etting go of the past is crucial for living a fulfilling life in the present. However, it is easier said than done. Memories, especially painful ones, tend to linger in our minds and haunt us. We may also hold on to past experiences, achievements, and failures, which can prevent us from moving forward. In this chapter, we will discuss why it's important to let go of the past and how to do it.

Living in the past can be detrimental to our mental health. We may feel stuck, unable to make progress, and experience negative emotions like guilt, regret, and resentment. We may also have unrealistic expectations of ourselves and others, based on past experiences. This can strain our relationships and create unnecessary stress. By holding on to the past, we are robbing ourselves of the chance to experience the joys of the present moment.

The first step towards letting go of the past is to acknowledge its hold on us. It's important to recognize that holding on to past experiences, whether good or bad, can prevent us from living in the present. We must identify the emotions and beliefs that are attached to the memories and experiences that we are holding on to. This can be difficult, as we may have become so accustomed to these feelings that we are unaware of their impact on our lives.

Once we have identified the emotions and beliefs that are holding us back, we must begin the process of releasing them. This involves accepting the past and acknowledging that it cannot be changed. We must learn to forgive ourselves and others for past mistakes and focus on what we can do now to make our lives better. We can't change the past, but we can change our present and future.

One effective way to let go of the past is to practice mindfulness. Mindfulness involves being present in the moment and observing our thoughts without judgment. This helps us to detach from our thoughts and emotions, allowing us to view them objectively. When we practice mindfulness, we can observe the thoughts and emotions that arise when we think about the past. We can then acknowledge them, accept them, and let them go.

Another way to let go of the past is to practice gratitude. Gratitude involves focusing on the positive aspects of our lives and expressing appreciation for them. By practicing gratitude, we can shift our focus from the past to the present and learn to appreciate what we have now. This can help us to let go of negative emotions and move on.

Finally, it's important to focus on the present and the future. We must set goals and work towards them, rather than dwelling on past achievements or failures. By focusing on the present and the future, we can create new experiences and memories that will replace the ones that we are holding on to. This can help us to move forward and live a more fulfilling life.

In conclusion, letting go of the past is essential for living in the present. It's important to recognize the impact that the past can have on our lives and identify the emotions and beliefs that are attached to it. By accepting the past, practicing mindfulness, gratitude, and focusing on the present and future, we can let go of negative emotions and experiences and create new, positive ones. We must learn to forgive ourselves and others, acknowledge our mistakes, and focus on making the present and future as fulfilling as possible. By letting go of the past, we can live in the moment and experience the joys of life.

The Art of Surrender: How to Find Peace in Letting Go

L etting go can be a difficult process, especially when we are used to being in control. However, surrendering to the present moment and accepting what we cannot change can be a powerful tool in finding inner peace and reducing stress and anxiety. In this chapter, we will explore the art of surrender and how to find peace in letting go.

Surrender is not the same as giving up or quitting. Rather, it is the act of acknowledging what we cannot control and releasing our attachment to it. This can be applied to many aspects of our lives, such as relationships, careers, and even our own thoughts and emotions. By surrendering, we let go of the struggle and resistance that can lead to stress and dissatisfaction.

One key aspect of surrender is acceptance. When we resist the present moment, we create tension within ourselves and prevent ourselves from experiencing inner peace. Accepting what is allows us to release the need to control and focus on what we can do to improve our situation. It doesn't mean we have to like or approve of what is happening, but it means we stop fighting against it and start working with it.

Another important aspect of surrender is trust. When we let go of our need to control, we open ourselves up to trusting the universe or a higher power to guide us on our path. This can be a scary concept, especially for those who are used to being in control, but it can be incredibly liberating. By trusting that everything is happening for a reason and that we are exactly where we need to be, we can let go of our worries and fears and focus on the present moment.

Surrender can also be applied to our relationships. When we hold on too tightly to people and our expectations of them, we can create tension and conflict. By surrendering our attachment to how we want others to be, we allow them to be themselves and focus on accepting and loving them as they are. This can lead to stronger, more authentic connections and a greater sense of inner peace.

Letting go and surrendering can also help us overcome difficult emotions such as anger, fear, and grief. When we try to control our emotions or resist them, we can create even more tension and anxiety. By surrendering to our emotions and accepting them as a natural part of the human experience, we can find inner peace and even a greater sense of self-awareness.

In conclusion, the art of surrender is a powerful tool for finding inner peace and reducing stress and anxiety. By accepting what we cannot control, trusting in the universe, and letting go of our attachments, we can find freedom and a greater sense of self-awareness. Remember that surrender is not the same as giving up or quitting, but rather an act of courage and trust in the present moment. Embrace the art of surrender and watch as your life transforms before your very eyes.

Letting Go of Expectations: The Liberation of Living in the Moment

L etting go of expectations can be one of the most liberating experiences a person can have. It allows us to live in the present moment and appreciate life for what it is, rather than constantly seeking something more. However, letting go of expectations is not always easy. It requires a conscious effort to change our mindset and embrace a new way of living.

Expectations are a natural part of life. We set goals for ourselves, create plans for the future, and have hopes and dreams. However, when our expectations become too rigid or unattainable, they can lead to disappointment, stress, and anxiety. The more we cling to our expectations, the more we limit ourselves and miss out on the joy and beauty of life as it is.

Letting go of expectations begins with understanding why we hold onto them in the first place. Often, our expectations are driven by societal pressures or external influences. We may feel the need to meet certain standards or live up to other people's expectations, whether they are real or imagined. Other times, our expectations are simply a way to try to control the uncontrollable. We cling to them as a way to create a sense of security in an uncertain world.

To let go of expectations, we must first become aware of them. We must be honest with ourselves and recognize when our expectations are limiting us or causing us unnecessary stress. Once we have identified our expectations, we can begin to challenge them. We can ask ourselves if they are realistic, if they are based on our own values and desires, or if they are coming from an external source.

Letting go of expectations also requires us to be more present in the moment. We must learn to appreciate what we have right now, rather than always focusing on what we want in the future. When we are present, we can see the beauty and joy in our lives as they are, rather than constantly searching for something more.

Learning to let go of expectations can be a difficult process, but the benefits are immeasurable. It allows us to live more freely and with less stress, to appreciate what we have in the present moment, and to be open to new experiences and opportunities. We may discover new passions, form deeper connections with those around us, and find a greater sense of purpose in our lives.

To let go of expectations, we must be willing to surrender control and embrace the unknown. We must be willing to take risks and be open to new experiences, even if they do not fit with our preconceived notions of how things should be. This requires a certain level of trust in ourselves and in the world around us.

In conclusion, letting go of expectations is a powerful way to live a more fulfilling and joyful life. It allows us to appreciate what we have in the present moment and to be open to new experiences and opportunities. It can be a difficult process, but the benefits are immeasurable. By learning to let go of our expectations, we can find a greater sense of peace and happiness in our lives.

The Power of Self-Forgiveness: How to Overcome Shame and Guilt

T he ability to forgive oneself is a powerful tool in the journey of letting go. When we hold onto feelings of shame and guilt, we can become trapped in our past mistakes, unable to move forward and find peace. Self-forgiveness allows us to release these negative emotions and open ourselves up to the possibility of a brighter future.

Often, we hold onto feelings of shame and guilt because we believe we have somehow failed ourselves or others. We may feel as though we should have acted differently, made better choices, or been a better person. However, the reality is that we all make mistakes. We are human, imperfect, and prone to error. Recognizing this truth is the first step towards self-forgiveness.

One of the most significant obstacles to self-forgiveness is the belief that we do not deserve it. We may feel as though we have committed a sin or crime that is unforgivable. However, the reality is that forgiveness is a choice. We can choose to forgive ourselves and release ourselves from the burden of our past mistakes. It is not about forgetting what we have done, but about accepting our mistakes and moving forward with a new perspective.

To begin the process of self-forgiveness, it is important to first acknowledge and take responsibility for our actions. We must own our mistakes and the consequences that came as a result of them. This may involve a deep sense of introspection and reflection, as we examine our actions and behaviors and try to understand what led us down that path.

Once we have taken responsibility for our actions, we can begin the process of self-forgiveness. This may involve seeking forgiveness from those we have hurt or wronged, but it is equally important to offer ourselves the same compassion and understanding. We must recognize that we are not defined by our mistakes and that we have the power to change and grow.

Self-forgiveness is a process that requires patience, self-compassion, and self-love. We must be willing to let go of our past mistakes and embrace the present moment. This may involve practicing self-care, seeking support from loved ones, or engaging in activities that bring us joy and fulfillment.

One helpful practice for self-forgiveness is to write a letter to ourselves, expressing our regrets and asking for forgiveness. We can then read this letter aloud, either to ourselves or to someone we trust. This practice can be a powerful tool for releasing negative emotions and finding a sense of closure.

It is important to remember that self-forgiveness is not a one-time event but an ongoing process. It may require multiple attempts, and we may find ourselves revisiting old feelings of shame and guilt from time to time. However, with practice, self-forgiveness can become a habit, allowing us to live more fully in the present moment and to let go of the past.

In conclusion, the power of self-forgiveness is a key component in the art of letting go. By learning to forgive ourselves, we can release ourselves from the burden of our past mistakes and open ourselves up to the possibility of a brighter future. Through self-compassion, patience, and self-love, we can find the courage to let go of shame and guilt and move forward with a sense of freedom and peace.

Letting Go of Envy: Finding Contentment in Our Own Lives

L etting go of envy can be a challenging task for many people, especially in today's world, where social media has made it easier than ever to compare ourselves to others. Envy is the feeling of wanting what someone else has, whether it be their material possessions, relationships, or personal qualities. While envy may seem like a natural human emotion, it can lead to negative consequences and hinder our own happiness and personal growth. In this chapter, we will explore the power of letting go of envy and finding contentment in our own lives.

Envy can cause us to feel inadequate and inferior, leading to feelings of frustration and discontentment. We may compare ourselves to others and feel as if we are not good enough or do not measure up to their achievements. This can lead to a negative self-image and low self-esteem, which can ultimately affect our relationships and overall well-being. Additionally, envy can lead to resentment towards others, creating tension in relationships and damaging our ability to connect with others.

To let go of envy, we need to focus on our own personal growth and achievements, rather than comparing ourselves to others. We should strive to live our own lives to the fullest and celebrate our own accomplishments, rather than feeling envious of the successes of others. This can be achieved by setting personal goals and working towards them, taking time to appreciate our own accomplishments, and practicing gratitude for what we have in our lives.

Practicing self-care is also an important step in letting go of envy. When we take care of ourselves, we are better able to focus on our own personal growth and well-being, rather than comparing ourselves to others. This can include activities such as exercise, meditation, and spending time with loved ones. By prioritizing self-care, we can strengthen our own self-worth and self-esteem, making it easier to let go of feelings of envy.

Another effective way to let go of envy is to practice empathy and compassion towards others. Rather than feeling jealous of someone else's accomplishments, we should try to understand and appreciate their journey. This can be achieved by putting ourselves in their shoes and acknowledging the challenges and hard work that they may have faced. Practicing empathy and compassion can also help to improve our relationships with others, as we are more likely to connect with them on a deeper level.

Letting go of envy also requires us to reframe our perspective. Instead of seeing the successes of others as a threat, we should view them as an inspiration. Rather than feeling envious, we can use their achievements as motivation to work towards our own goals and aspirations. This mindset shift can help us to let go of negative feelings and focus on our own personal growth and development.

Ultimately, letting go of envy requires us to find contentment in our own lives. This can be achieved by embracing who we are, appreciating our own unique qualities, and recognizing that our worth is not defined by our achievements or material possessions. By finding contentment within ourselves, we can let go of the need to compare ourselves to others and focus on our own personal growth and happiness.

In conclusion, letting go of envy can be a powerful tool for personal growth and happiness. By focusing on our own personal growth and achievements, practicing self-care, empathy, and compassion, reframing our perspective, and finding contentment within ourselves, we can let go of envy and find contentment in our own lives. By doing so, we can strengthen our relationships, improve our overall well-being, and live a more fulfilling life.

The Art of Acceptance: How to Embrace What Is and Let Go of What Isn't

The journey of letting go begins with acceptance. It can be difficult to let go of things that we can't control, but learning to accept what is and let go of what isn't can be incredibly liberating. Acceptance is not about giving up, but rather about acknowledging the reality of a situation and choosing to move forward from a place of inner peace and contentment.

One of the biggest challenges of acceptance is recognizing that not everything will go as planned. Life is unpredictable and full of surprises, and it's important to understand that sometimes things will not turn out the way we expected. When we resist this reality and hold onto expectations, we create unnecessary stress and anxiety for ourselves.

Learning to accept what is and let go of what isn't begins with acknowledging our emotions. It's important to give ourselves permission to feel our feelings, whether they are positive or negative. Suppressing our emotions can prevent us from moving forward and finding acceptance. It's okay to feel disappointed or sad when things don't go as planned. The key is to acknowledge these emotions, accept them, and then let them go.

Another important aspect of acceptance is cultivating a sense of gratitude. When we focus on what we have rather than what we lack, we are able to find contentment in the present moment. Gratitude is not about denying the difficulties of life, but rather about finding joy and meaning despite them.

Letting go of what isn't is not about giving up on our goals or aspirations, but rather about acknowledging what is within our control and what is not. We may not be able to control the actions of others, for example, but we can control our own reactions to their actions. It's important to recognize the difference and focus on what we can do, rather than what we can't.

Learning to let go of what isn't also means learning to trust the process of life. Sometimes the universe has a plan for us that we can't yet see, and it's important to trust that everything will work out as it's meant to. When we let go of the need for control, we open ourselves up to new possibilities and opportunities that we may have otherwise overlooked.

Ultimately, the art of acceptance is about finding inner peace and contentment. When we learn to accept what is and let go of what isn't, we free ourselves from the burden of expectations and create space for new experiences and growth. It's not always easy, but the rewards are significant. By cultivating acceptance, we are able to live more fully in the present moment and appreciate the beauty of life, even in the midst of chaos and uncertainty.

In conclusion, the art of acceptance is about finding the balance between acknowledging the reality of a situation and letting go of expectations. It's about embracing what is and finding contentment in the present moment, while also acknowledging that we have the power to shape our own futures. By learning to let go of what isn't and trust the process of life, we are able to find inner peace and live more fully in the present.

Letting Go of Negative Self-Talk: How to Find Self-Love and Confidence

Our minds can be both our greatest ally and our worst enemy. When we let negative self-talk take over, we can easily slip into a spiral of self-doubt and insecurity. This can hold us back from realizing our full potential and living a happy, fulfilling life. But the good news is that we have the power to change our thoughts and let go of the negativity.

Negative self-talk can take many forms, such as self-criticism, self-doubt, and negative self-judgment. It's the voice in our head that tells us we're not good enough, we're not capable, or we don't deserve success. This can lead to feelings of anxiety, depression, and low self-esteem. But the truth is, these thoughts are often based on false beliefs and assumptions that we've internalized over time.

One of the first steps to letting go of negative self-talk is to become aware of when it's happening. Pay attention to your thoughts and notice when they start to turn negative. Once you recognize the negative self-talk, you can challenge it with positive self-talk. This can be as simple as replacing a negative thought with a positive one, such as "I can't do this" with "I am capable and competent."

Another way to let go of negative self-talk is to practice self-compassion. This means treating ourselves with the same kindness and understanding that we would offer to a close friend. Instead of criticizing ourselves for our flaws and mistakes, we can choose to be kind and supportive. We can remind ourselves that we are human and that making mistakes is a natural part of life.

One effective technique for letting go of negative self-talk is to reframe our thoughts. This means looking at a situation from a different perspective and focusing on the positive aspects. For example, instead of beating yourself up for making a mistake, you can view it as a learning opportunity and a chance to grow. This can help you shift your focus from self-criticism to self-improvement.

It's also important to remember that our thoughts are not necessarily facts. Just because we think something about ourselves doesn't mean it's true. We can challenge our negative self-talk by asking ourselves if there is evidence to support our beliefs. Often, we'll find that there isn't. This can help us let go of the negative thoughts and move on to more positive ones.

Another helpful technique is to practice gratitude. When we focus on what we're grateful for, we shift our attention away from the negative and toward the positive. This can help us cultivate a more positive mindset and let go of negative self-talk. We can start by making a list of things we're grateful for each day, no matter how small.

Finally, it's important to take care of ourselves in other ways. When we're stressed, tired, or overwhelmed, it can be harder to maintain a positive mindset. We can let go of negative self-talk by taking care of our physical, emotional, and mental health. This can include getting enough sleep, eating healthy foods, exercising, practicing mindfulness, and seeking support from loved ones or a professional if needed.

Letting go of negative self-talk takes practice and patience. But with time, we can learn to recognize when it's happening and replace it with positive self-talk. This can help us feel more confident, self-assured, and empowered to live the life we want. By letting go of negative self-talk, we can find self-love and confidence and truly thrive.

Finding Freedom in Minimalism: How to Let Go of Material Possessions

In today's world, we are constantly surrounded by advertisements and social media messages that urge us to buy more, have more, and accumulate more. Our homes are filled with countless possessions that we often don't need or even use, yet we hold onto them because we believe they define us, give us security, or bring us happiness. However, the reality is that this accumulation of stuff can create clutter in our homes and in our minds, leading to stress, anxiety, and even depression. The solution to this is minimalism, a lifestyle that is all about living with less and finding freedom in simplicity.

The first step towards minimalism is to evaluate what we really need in our lives. What is essential and what is simply clutter? This can be a daunting task, but it is essential to find clarity and identify the possessions that truly add value to our lives. We can start by decluttering one room at a time, setting aside anything that we haven't used in the past year or that doesn't bring us joy. It is important to be honest with ourselves and let go of items that we are holding onto for sentimental or emotional reasons. We should focus on keeping only the things that we truly need and cherish.

It is also important to recognize that minimalism is not just about decluttering our physical space, but also our mental space. This means letting go of negative thoughts and beliefs that are holding us back. We need to practice mindfulness and focus on the present moment, rather than dwelling on the past or worrying about the future. This can be achieved through meditation, journaling, or other forms of self-reflection.

One of the benefits of minimalism is that it allows us to be more intentional with our spending. Instead of mindlessly consuming and accumulating, we can focus on purchasing items that truly add value to our lives. This can be liberating, as it frees us from the pressure to keep up with the latest trends or to impress others with our possessions. It also allows us to save money and invest in experiences that truly bring us joy, such as traveling, pursuing hobbies, or spending time with loved ones.

Minimalism can also help us develop a greater appreciation for the simple things in life. By letting go of our attachment to material possessions, we can find joy in the everyday moments, such as spending time in nature, enjoying a good book, or having a meaningful conversation with a friend. This can lead to a greater sense of contentment and fulfillment in life, as we learn to appreciate what we have rather than constantly striving for more.

Of course, minimalism is not for everyone, and it is important to recognize that we all have different needs and values. However, by embracing minimalism, we can find a sense of freedom and liberation that comes from letting go of the things that no longer serve us. We can create space in our homes and our minds, allowing us to focus on what is truly important and to live a life that is in alignment with our values.

In conclusion, minimalism is not just about having less; it's about living more intentionally and finding freedom in simplicity. By letting go of material possessions, negative thoughts, and attachments to what no longer serves us, we can create space for the things that truly matter. This can lead to a greater sense of contentment, fulfillment, and joy in our lives.

The Art of Moving On: How to Start Fresh and Embrace the Future

The end of one chapter in life often marks the beginning of a new one. Whether it's leaving a job, a relationship, a home, or even a city, starting fresh can be both exhilarating and daunting. But with the right mindset and approach, it's possible to move on from the past and embrace the future.

One of the first steps in moving on is acknowledging and processing the emotions associated with the change. It's natural to feel a sense of loss or grief when letting go of something that was once familiar or important. However, it's important to remember that change is a normal and necessary part of life. Instead of dwelling on what's lost, focus on the possibilities and opportunities that lie ahead.

Another key component of moving on is letting go of any negative thoughts or beliefs that may be holding you back. This could include self-doubt, fear, or limiting beliefs. One way to overcome these barriers is to practice positive self-talk and visualization. Focus on the things you want to achieve, rather than what you're leaving behind. Believe in your ability to create the life you want and take steps towards making it a reality.

It's also important to surround yourself with positive influences and supportive people. Seek out friends, family members, or mentors who can offer encouragement, advice, or even just a listening ear. Building a strong support system can help you stay motivated and optimistic, even in the face of challenges.

Another helpful strategy for moving on is to create a clear plan or roadmap for your future. This could involve setting specific goals, creating a vision board, or even just writing out your priorities and values. Having a sense of direction and purpose can help you feel more empowered and focused as you move forward.

Finally, it's important to take care of yourself during this time of transition. This could mean focusing on self-care activities like exercise, meditation, or hobbies that bring you joy. It could also mean seeking professional help if you're struggling with mental health concerns like anxiety or depression. Remember that it's okay to ask for help when you need it, and that taking care of yourself is a crucial part of moving on and building a happy, fulfilling life.

In many ways, moving on is an art form. It requires a combination of self-reflection, positive thinking, and practical planning. But by taking intentional steps to let go of the past and embrace the future, it's possible to find freedom and joy in the present. Embrace the possibilities that come with change, and trust in your own ability to create a happy and fulfilling life. The future is full of possibilities – it's up to you to seize them.

Letting Go of Resilience: How to Find Strength in Vulnerability

Letting go of the belief that we must always be resilient can be difficult, but it can also be incredibly freeing. We often think of resilience as a positive trait, something to aspire to. After all, we admire those who are able to weather any storm and bounce back from adversity. However, the idea of always being resilient can also be harmful, as it can lead us to suppress our emotions and neglect our needs.

When we try to be resilient all the time, we may feel like we can't show vulnerability. We may think that we need to keep up a façade of strength, even when we're struggling. This can lead to feelings of isolation, as we may not feel comfortable reaching out to others for help. It can also cause us to neglect our own needs, as we may think that taking time for self-care is a sign of weakness.

Learning to let go of the need to be resilient all the time can be a powerful step towards finding strength in vulnerability. This doesn't mean that we should stop striving for resilience altogether; rather, it means recognizing that vulnerability is also a form of strength. When we allow ourselves to be vulnerable, we open ourselves up to the possibility of growth and connection.

One way to let go of the need to be resilient all the time is to practice self-compassion. We can start by acknowledging that we all have weaknesses and flaws, and that it's okay to struggle at times. Instead of beating ourselves up for not being able to handle everything perfectly, we can learn to treat ourselves with kindness and understanding.

Another way to find strength in vulnerability is to reach out to others for support. When we allow ourselves to be vulnerable with others, we give them the opportunity to show us empathy and support. This can be difficult, as it requires us to let down our guard and show our true selves. But when we allow ourselves to be vulnerable with others, we build stronger connections and create a sense of community.

Finally, it's important to recognize that vulnerability is not a weakness. In fact, vulnerability can be a powerful tool for personal growth and development. When we allow ourselves to be vulnerable, we create space for new experiences and new ways of thinking. We may discover that there are things we're passionate about that we never would have known about if we hadn't been open to vulnerability.

Letting go of the need to be resilient all the time can be a scary prospect. We may worry that we'll be seen as weak or that we won't be able to handle things if we're not always strong. But by letting go of this need, we create space for growth, connection, and self-discovery. We allow ourselves to be fully human, with all of the imperfections and weaknesses that come with that. And in doing so, we may discover a newfound sense of strength and resilience that comes from embracing vulnerability.

The Art of Letting Go of Busyness: Why We Need Rest and Reflection

In today's fast-paced world, busyness is often celebrated and rewarded. Many of us wear our busyness as a badge of honor, equating it with productivity and success. But what happens when we become so consumed by our busyness that we neglect our physical and emotional needs? This is where the art of letting go of busyness comes in.

Busyness can take many forms, from work-related tasks to social obligations to personal responsibilities. We often fill our schedules to the brim, leaving little time for rest and relaxation. This constant state of busyness can lead to physical and emotional exhaustion, burnout, and even illness.

Letting go of busyness is not about becoming lazy or unproductive. Instead, it is about finding a healthy balance between activity and rest. It is about learning to prioritize our needs and to recognize when we are pushing ourselves too hard.

The first step in letting go of busyness is to acknowledge the negative impact it is having on our lives. We need to be honest with ourselves about how our busyness is affecting our physical health, emotional well-being, and relationships. We must recognize that our productivity does not define our worth, and that rest and reflection are just as important as activity.

Once we have acknowledged the negative impact of our busyness, we can start to take action to let it go. This may involve saying no to certain obligations, delegating tasks to others, or setting boundaries around our time. It may also involve carving out time for rest and reflection, such as taking a walk in nature, meditating, or journaling.

It is important to remember that letting go of busyness is not a one-time event. It is an ongoing process that requires us to be mindful of our schedules and our priorities. We may need to reassess our commitments on a regular basis and make adjustments as needed.

When we let go of busyness, we create space for rest, reflection, and creativity. We give ourselves permission to slow down and enjoy the present moment. We also open ourselves up to new opportunities and experiences that we may have otherwise missed.

Letting go of busyness can also have a positive impact on our relationships. When we are not consumed by our to-do lists, we can be more present with our loved ones and more engaged in our interactions with them. We can also be more empathetic and understanding when others are feeling overwhelmed.

In addition to the benefits of rest and reflection, letting go of busyness can also lead to increased productivity and creativity. When we are not constantly rushing from one task to the next, we have the mental space to think more deeply and creatively about the work we are doing. We may also find that we are able to accomplish more in less time because we are more focused and energized.

In conclusion, the art of letting go of busyness is an important skill that can help us find balance, rest, and renewal in our lives. By acknowledging the negative impact of our busyness, taking action to let it go, and creating space for rest and reflection, we can improve our physical and emotional well-being, enhance our relationships, and increase our productivity and creativity. Letting go of busyness is not about becoming lazy or unproductive, but about finding a healthy balance between activity and rest.

The Power of Letting Go of the Need for Approval: How to Live Authentically

The need for approval is a natural human tendency. From childhood, we learn to seek validation and recognition from our parents, teachers, and peers. As we grow older, this need can evolve into a strong desire for external validation from our bosses, colleagues, friends, and romantic partners. While seeking approval can help us feel valued and accepted, it can also become a trap that hinders our growth, and limits our ability to live authentically. In this chapter, we will explore the power of letting go of the need for approval and how it can help us live a more fulfilling and authentic life.

One of the main reasons why we seek approval is because we fear rejection. We worry that if we don't meet the expectations of others, we will be rejected, judged, or ostracized. This fear can be paralyzing and can prevent us from pursuing our dreams or being true to ourselves. We may compromise our values, beliefs, and desires to conform to what we think others want from us. However, living our lives based on the expectations of others can leave us feeling empty and unfulfilled.

Letting go of the need for approval starts with developing a strong sense of self-awareness. We need to be honest with ourselves about who we are, what we want, and what we value. It's essential to take the time to reflect on our lives and our choices, and to ask ourselves whether they align with our values and beliefs. When we have a clear sense of who we are, we are less likely to seek approval from others, as we are already secure in ourselves.

Another way to let go of the need for approval is to focus on our inner voice rather than external validation. We can cultivate a strong sense of self-esteem and confidence by recognizing and celebrating our strengths and accomplishments. Instead of seeking praise or recognition from others, we can learn to appreciate ourselves and acknowledge our successes. By valuing ourselves, we become less reliant on external validation and can make decisions based on what feels right for us.

Letting go of the need for approval also means learning to embrace our uniqueness. We need to recognize that we are all different, and that's what makes us special. Rather than trying to fit into a mold created by others, we can embrace our individuality and find the courage to be ourselves. This may involve taking risks, making mistakes, and even facing criticism from others. However, when we learn to embrace our true selves, we can live a more authentic and fulfilling life.

It's also important to surround ourselves with people who support us and accept us for who we are. By building relationships based on authenticity and mutual respect, we can find a sense of belonging and connection without sacrificing our identity. When we have people in our lives who love us for who we are, we don't need to seek approval from others.

Finally, letting go of the need for approval requires us to accept that we cannot control what others think or feel about us. We can't control their opinions, reactions, or expectations. What we can control is how we react and respond to those opinions. By developing a strong sense of self-worth and resilience, we can learn to handle criticism and rejection with grace and compassion.

In conclusion, letting go of the need for approval is a powerful step towards living a more authentic and fulfilling life. It requires developing a strong sense of self-awareness, building self-esteem, embracing our uniqueness, and surrounding ourselves with supportive relationships. By accepting ourselves for who we are, we can find the courage to pursue our dreams and make decisions based on what feels right for us. We can also learn to handle criticism and rejection with resilience and compassion. When we let go of the need for approval, we find the freedom to live a life that is true to ourselves.

Finding Your Purpose in Letting Go: How to Align Your Life with Your Values

Letting go is often associated with loss, but it can also be a powerful tool for gaining clarity and direction in life. When we let go of things that no longer serve us, we create space for new opportunities and experiences to come our way. This includes the pursuit of finding one's purpose in life. Many people feel stuck or unfulfilled because they are unsure of their life's purpose. However, letting go of certain beliefs, habits, or people can be the catalyst for discovering one's true calling.

To begin this process, it is important to reflect on one's values and passions. Ask yourself what brings you joy and fulfillment, what makes you feel alive, and what impact you want to make in the world. These questions will help you gain clarity on what you want to prioritize in your life and what you are willing to let go of to achieve your goals.

Letting go can be a scary process, as it often involves taking risks and stepping outside of one's comfort zone. However, it is important to remember that pursuing one's purpose is not meant to be easy, and it often requires sacrifices and hard work. It is important to stay focused on the end goal and trust in the process, even when it feels uncertain or uncomfortable.

One of the biggest obstacles to finding one's purpose is fear. Fear of failure, fear of the unknown, and fear of judgment can all prevent us from taking the necessary steps towards living a fulfilling life. However, it is important to acknowledge these fears and work through them in order to move forward. Letting go of the need for perfection and embracing the journey, even with its bumps and setbacks, can be a powerful tool in finding one's purpose.

Another important aspect of finding one's purpose is surrounding oneself with a supportive community. This can include friends, family, mentors, or like-minded individuals who can provide encouragement and guidance along the way. It is important to let go of relationships or environments that hold you back from your goals and seek out those that challenge and inspire you to grow.

It is also important to let go of limiting beliefs and self-doubt that can prevent us from pursuing our purpose. The belief that we are not good enough, smart enough, or talented enough can hold us back from taking risks and pursuing our dreams. However, it is important to challenge these beliefs and instead focus on our strengths and abilities.

The process of finding one's purpose is not a one-time event but rather an ongoing journey. As we continue to let go of things that no longer serve us and pursue our passions and goals, we will likely encounter new challenges and opportunities that require us to reevaluate and adjust our course. It is important to stay open-minded and flexible and trust in our intuition and inner voice.

In conclusion, letting go can be a powerful tool in finding one's purpose. By letting go of things that no longer serve us and pursuing our passions and values, we create space for new opportunities and experiences to come our way. This process requires courage, resilience, and self-awareness, but the rewards can be immeasurable. Letting go of limiting beliefs, fears, and toxic relationships, and cultivating a supportive community and positive mindset can all contribute to discovering one's purpose and living a fulfilling life.

The Art of Letting Go of What Others Think: How to Find Your Voice and Be Yourself

The fear of judgment and rejection is a common challenge that many of us face when it comes to being true to ourselves. We often try to mold ourselves into what we believe others want us to be, whether it's at work, with friends, or in social situations. However, living your life according to other people's expectations is not fulfilling or sustainable. It's important to let go of the need for approval and find the courage to be yourself.

One of the biggest obstacles to letting go of what others think is the fear of being judged. We often worry that if we reveal our true selves, we will be criticized or rejected. It's important to remember that we can't control how others perceive us, and that their opinions are not a reflection of our worth or value. The only person whose opinion truly matters is ourselves. When we learn to let go of the need for external validation, we can begin to focus on our own happiness and fulfillment.

Another key step in letting go of what others think is to identify and embrace our core values. What is important to us, and what do we stand for? When we are clear on our values, it becomes easier to make choices that align with them, and to let go of the opinions of others that don't serve us. For example, if we value creativity and self-expression, we may choose to pursue a career in the arts, even if others believe that it's not a practical choice.

Letting go of the need for approval also involves embracing vulnerability. When we are authentic and genuine, we expose ourselves to the possibility of rejection or criticism. However, vulnerability also allows us to connect with others on a deeper level and to experience true intimacy and understanding. By letting go of the need to protect ourselves from the opinions of others, we open ourselves up to deeper and more fulfilling relationships.

It's also important to recognize that letting go of what others think is a process, not a one-time event. We will likely face moments of doubt and fear along the way, but with practice, we can become more comfortable with our true selves. We may find that some relationships are no longer compatible with our values or our sense of self, and that's okay. It's better to be true to ourselves and let go of those who don't support us than to try to fit into someone else's expectations.

In order to let go of what others think, we must also let go of our own judgments and expectations of ourselves. It's common to hold ourselves to impossibly high standards, and to criticize ourselves for perceived flaws or shortcomings. By practicing self-compassion and self-love, we can begin to let go of negative self-talk and embrace our strengths and abilities. When we feel good about ourselves, we are less likely to be affected by the opinions of others.

In conclusion, the art of letting go of what others think is a process of self-discovery and self-acceptance. It involves identifying and embracing our core values, practicing vulnerability and authenticity, and letting go of negative self-talk and judgments. When we let go of the need for approval, we can focus on our own happiness and fulfillment, and develop deeper and more meaningful relationships with those who support and accept us for who we truly are. It takes courage and practice, but the freedom that comes with living authentically is well worth the effort.

Don't miss out!

Visit the website below and you can sign up to receive emails whenever Barbara Smith publishes a new book. There's no charge and no obligation.

https://books2read.com/r/B-A-FWIR-EZVFC

BOOKS 2 READ

Connecting independent readers to independent writers.

Also by Barbara Smith

About the Publisher

Accepting manuscripts in the most categories. We love to help people get their words available to the world.

Revival Waves of Glory focus is to provide more options to be published. We do traditional paperbacks, hardcovers, audio books and ebooks all over the world. A traditional royalty-based publisher that offers self-publishing options, Revival Waves provides a very author friendly and transparent publishing process, with President Bill Vincent involved in the full process of your book. Send us your manuscript and we will contact you as soon as possible.

Contact: Bill Vincent at rwgpublishing@yahoo.com